Vol 15

MAZE

FOR KIDS

Ages 4-6

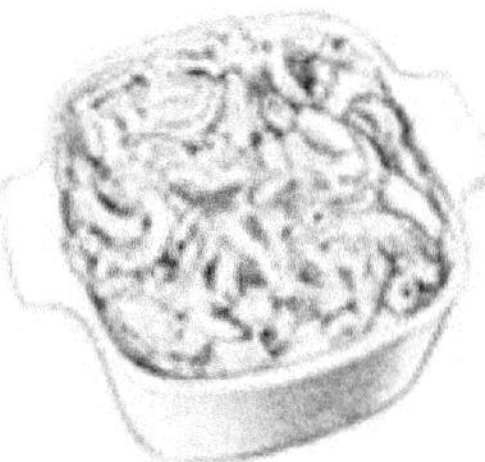

MAZE BOOK

SOCIAL MEDIA

- /MySweetBooks1
- /MySweetBooks1
- /MySweetBooks1
- /MySweetBooks

Email Us : mysweetbooks1@gmail.com

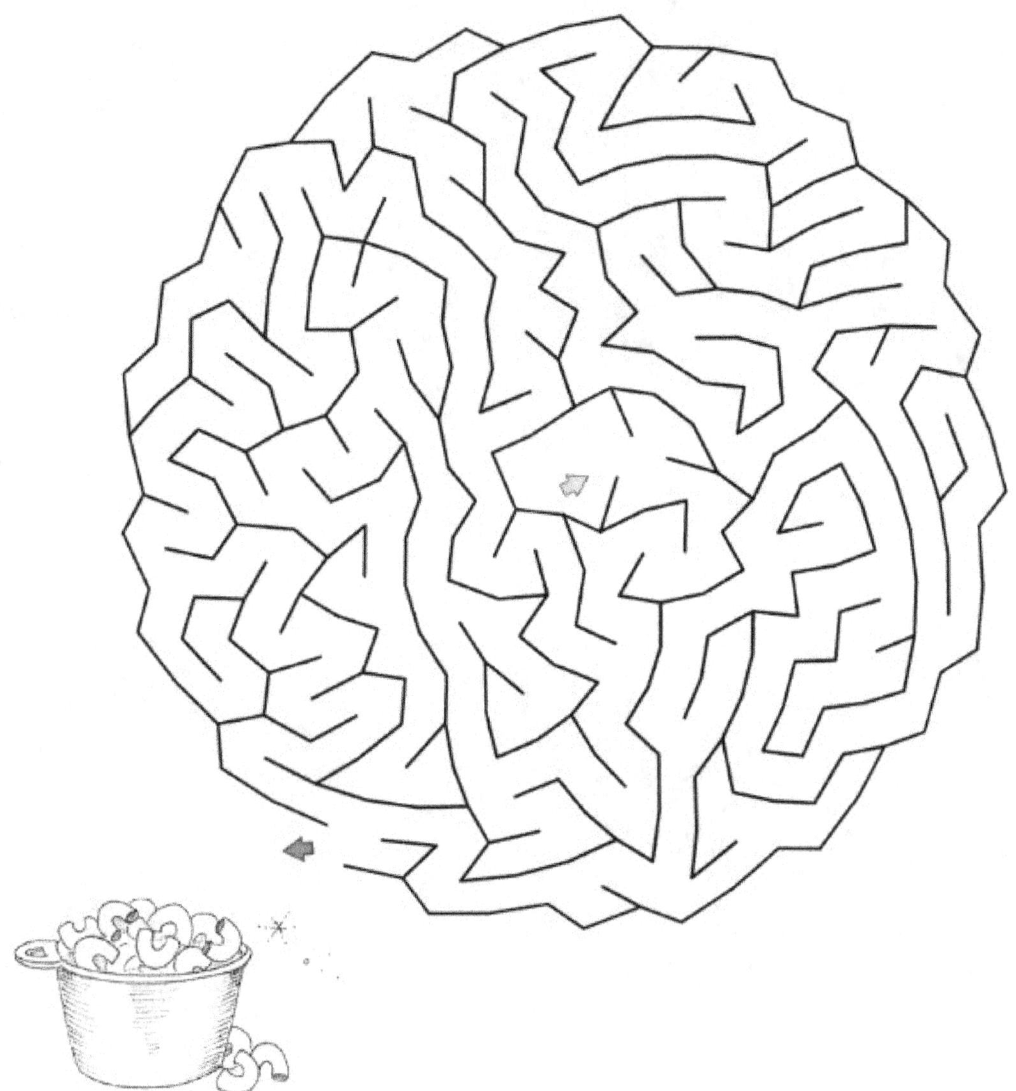

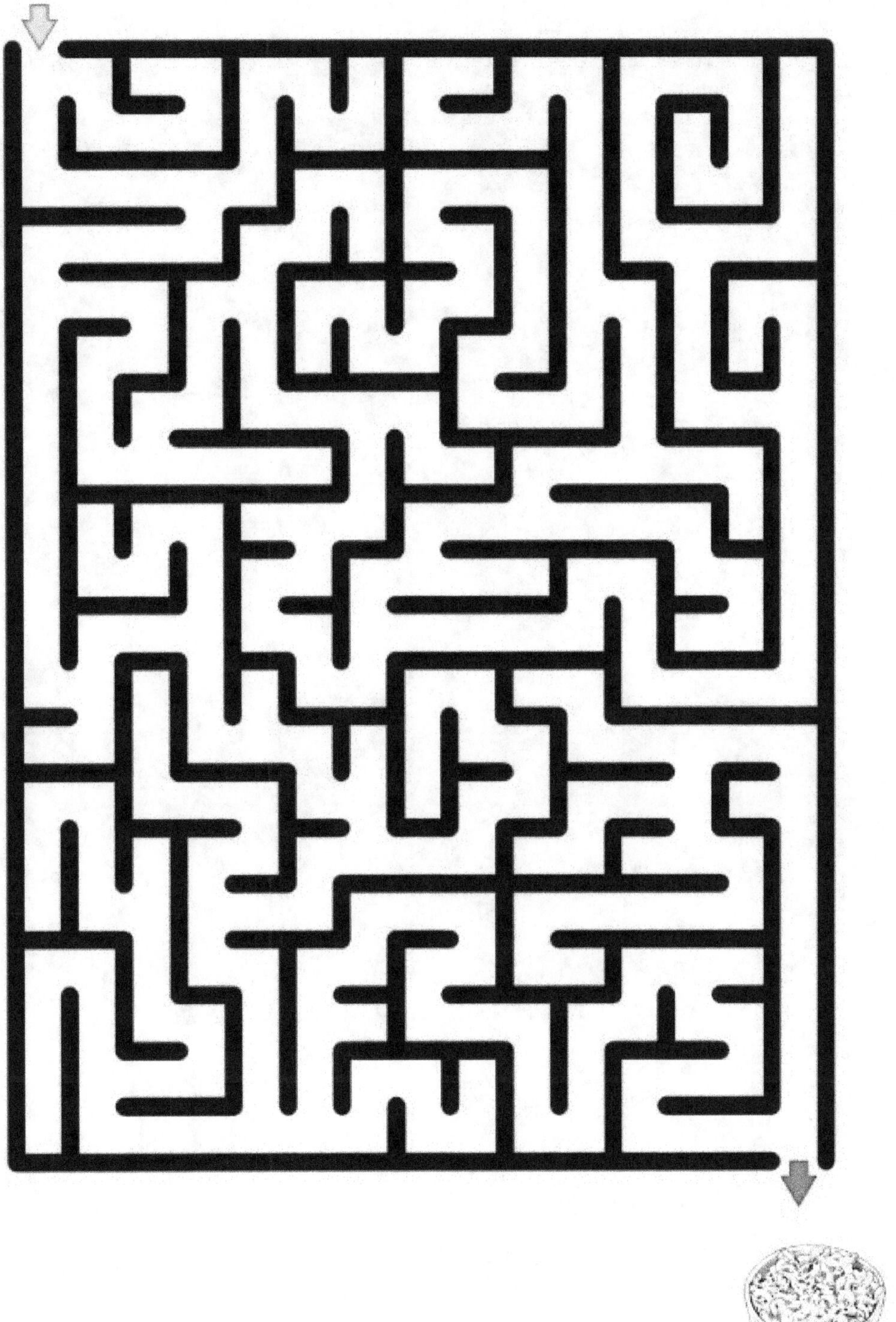

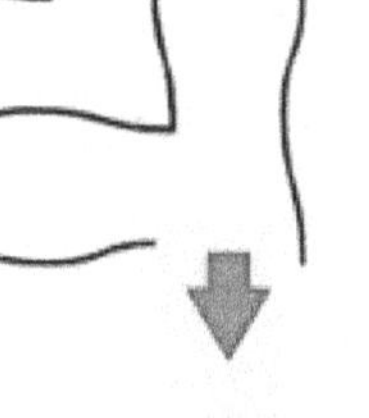

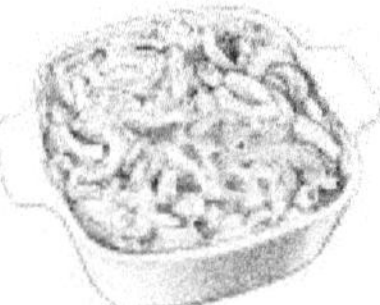

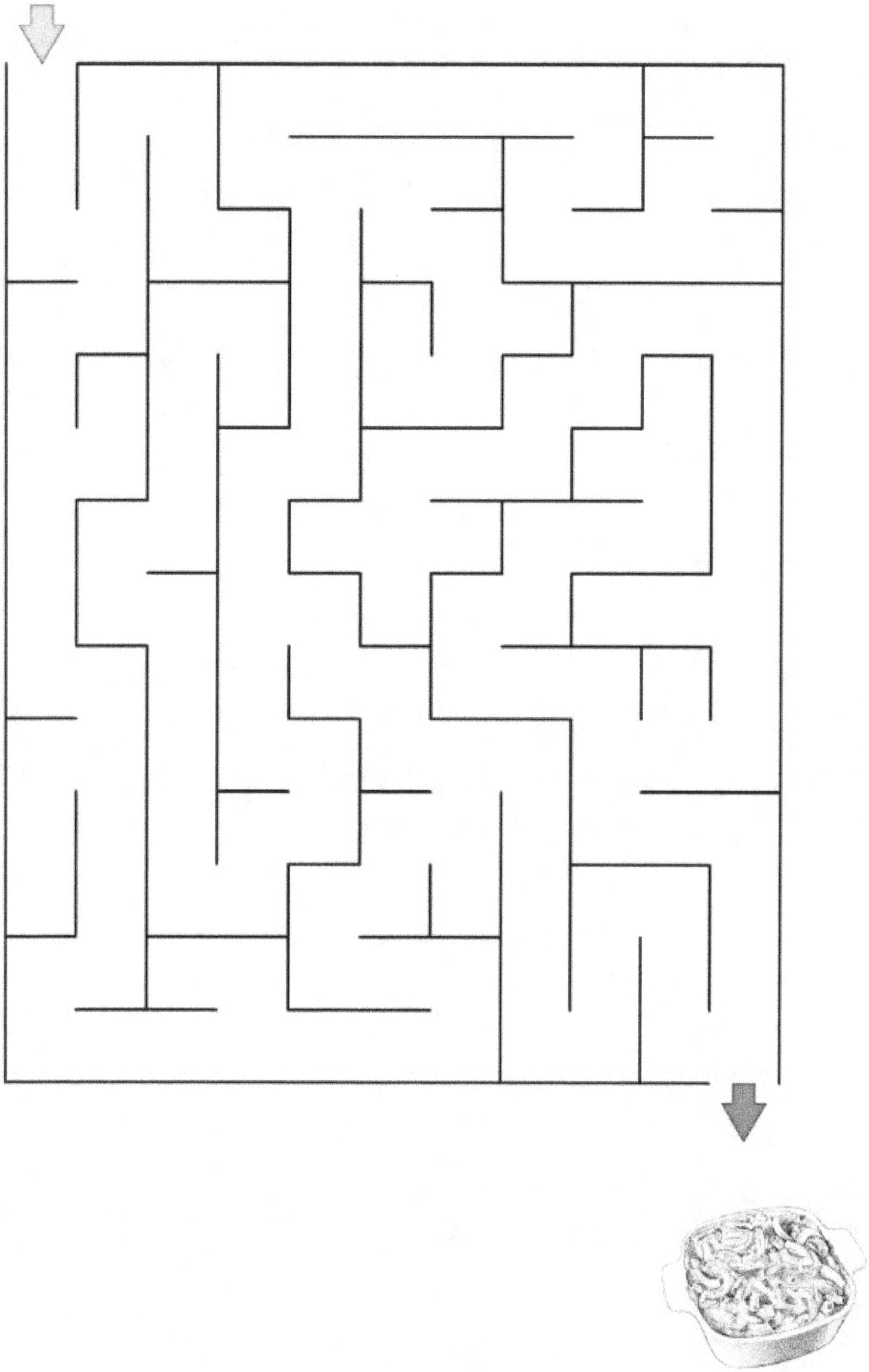

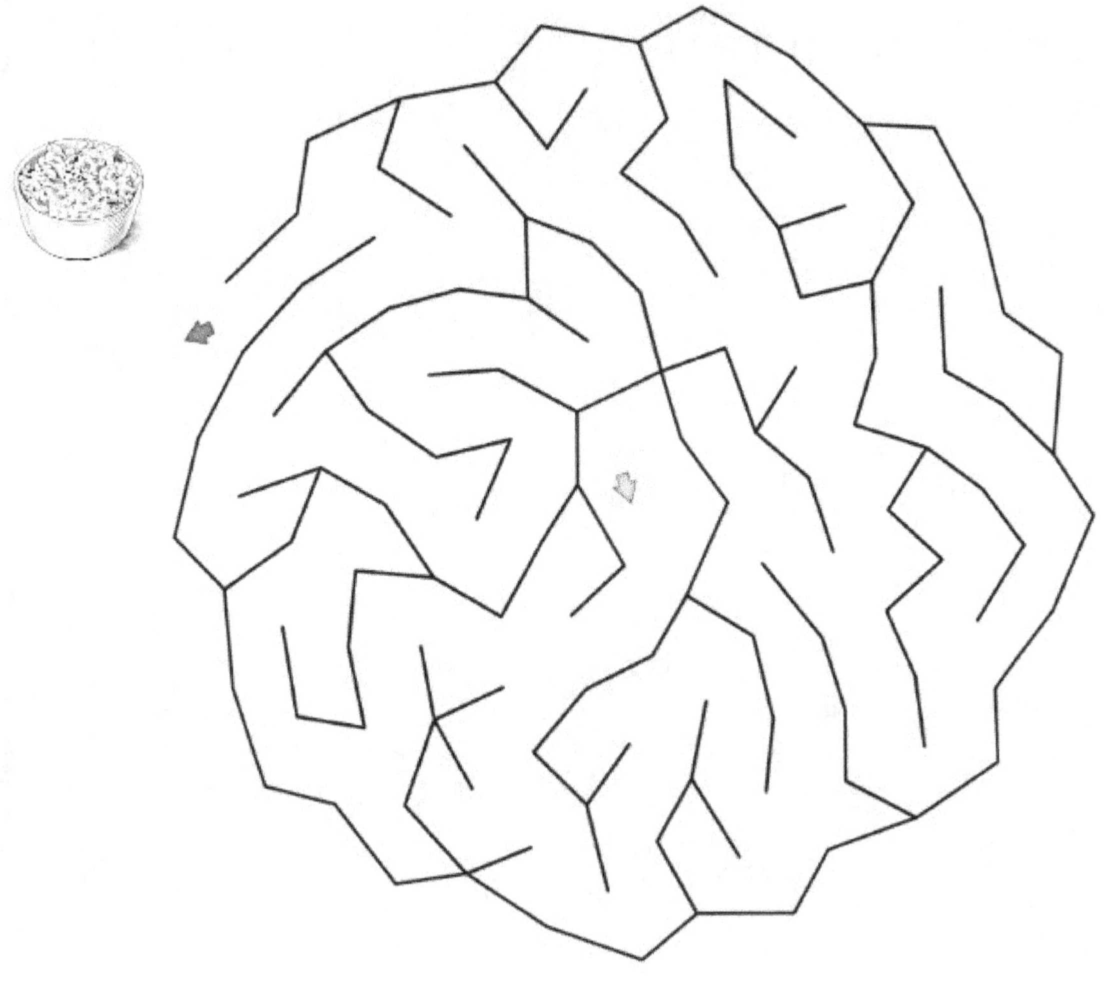

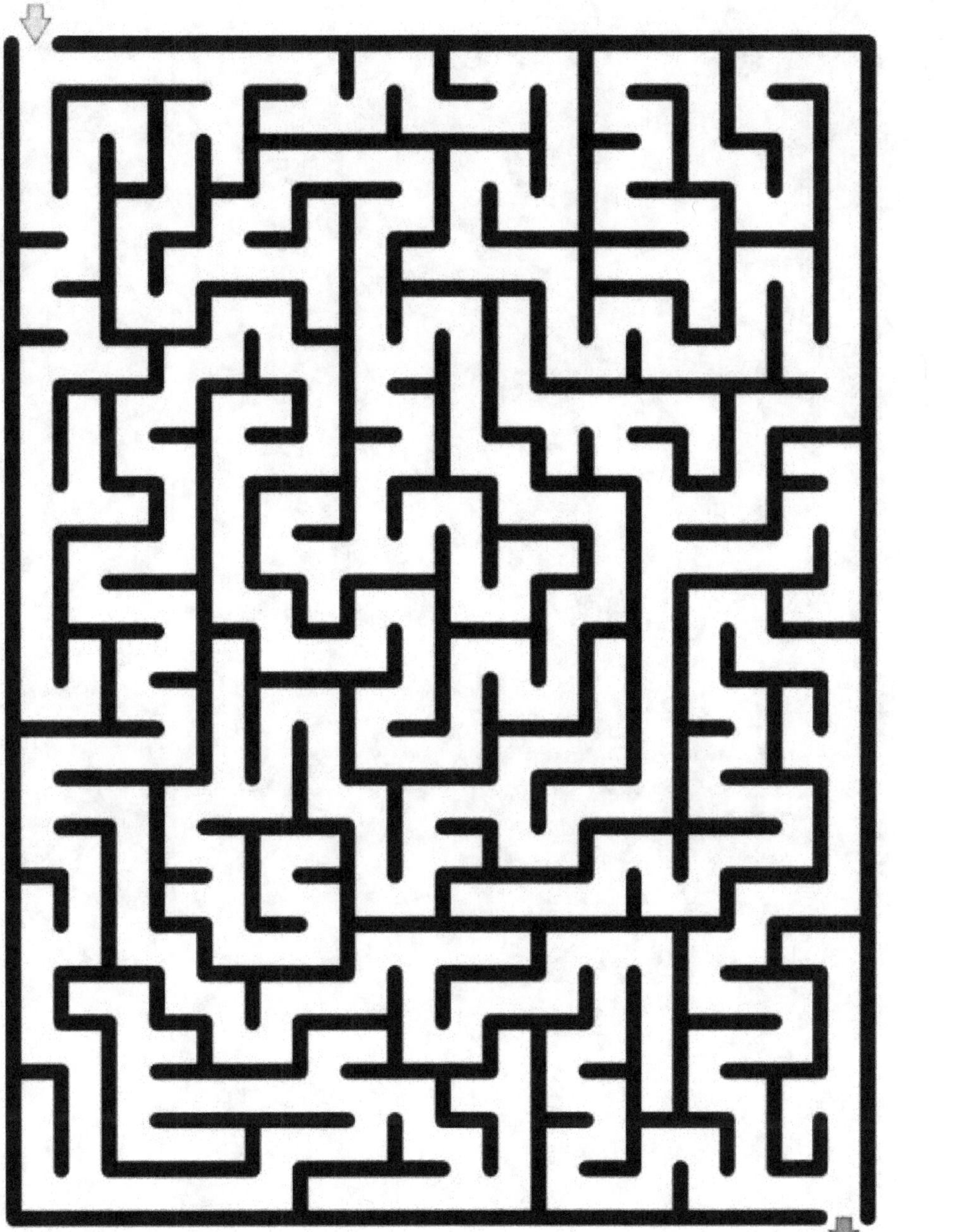

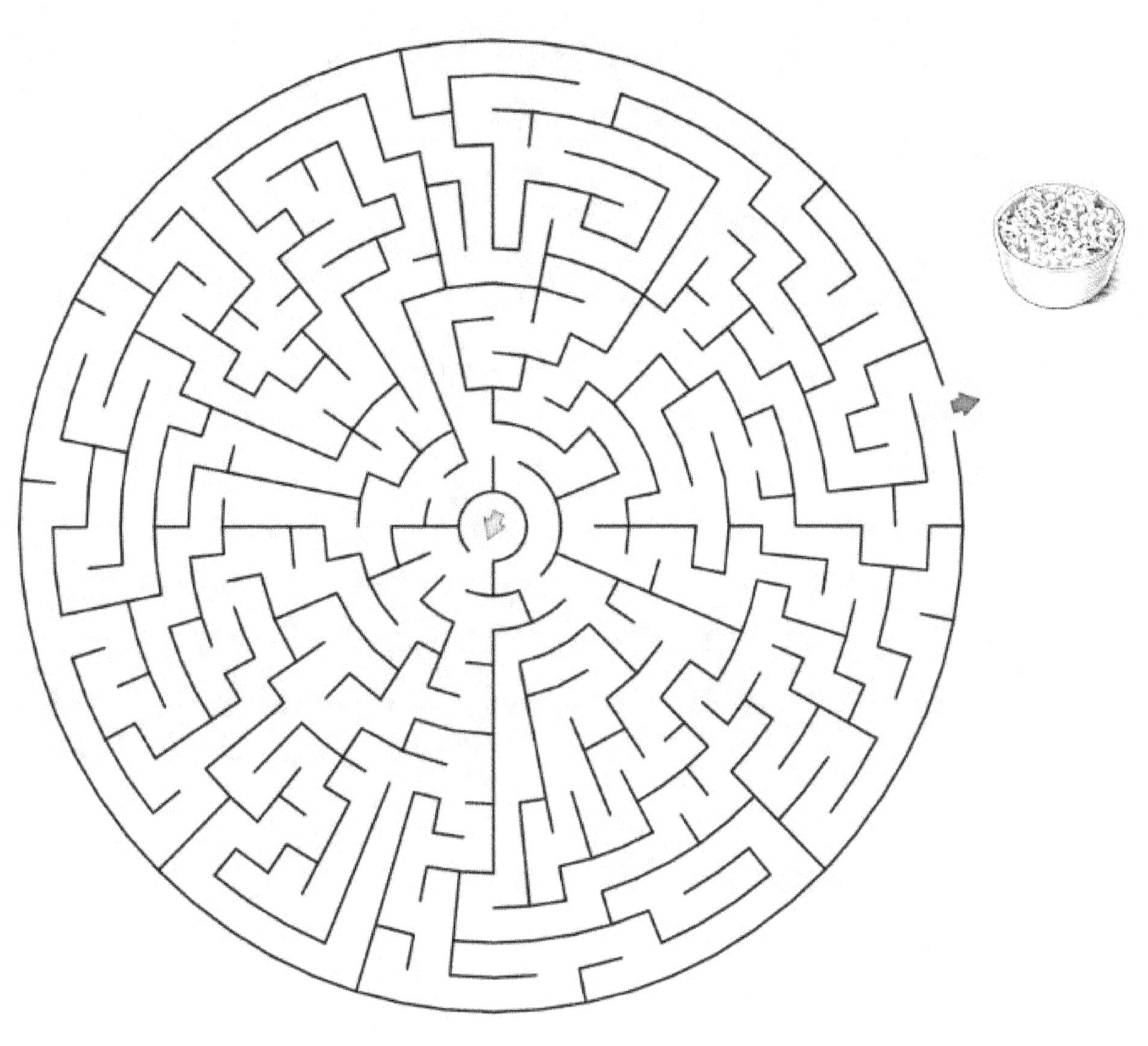

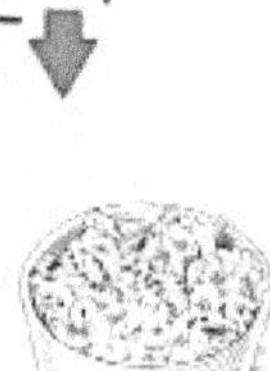

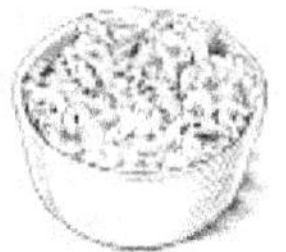

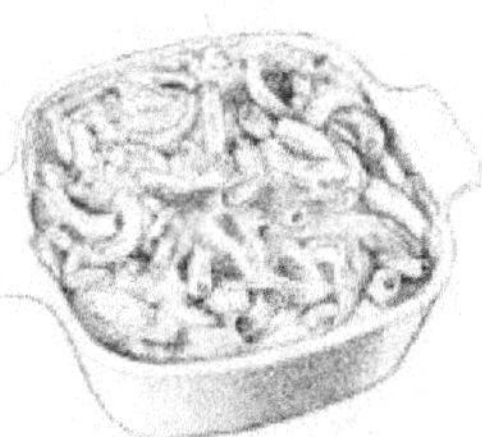

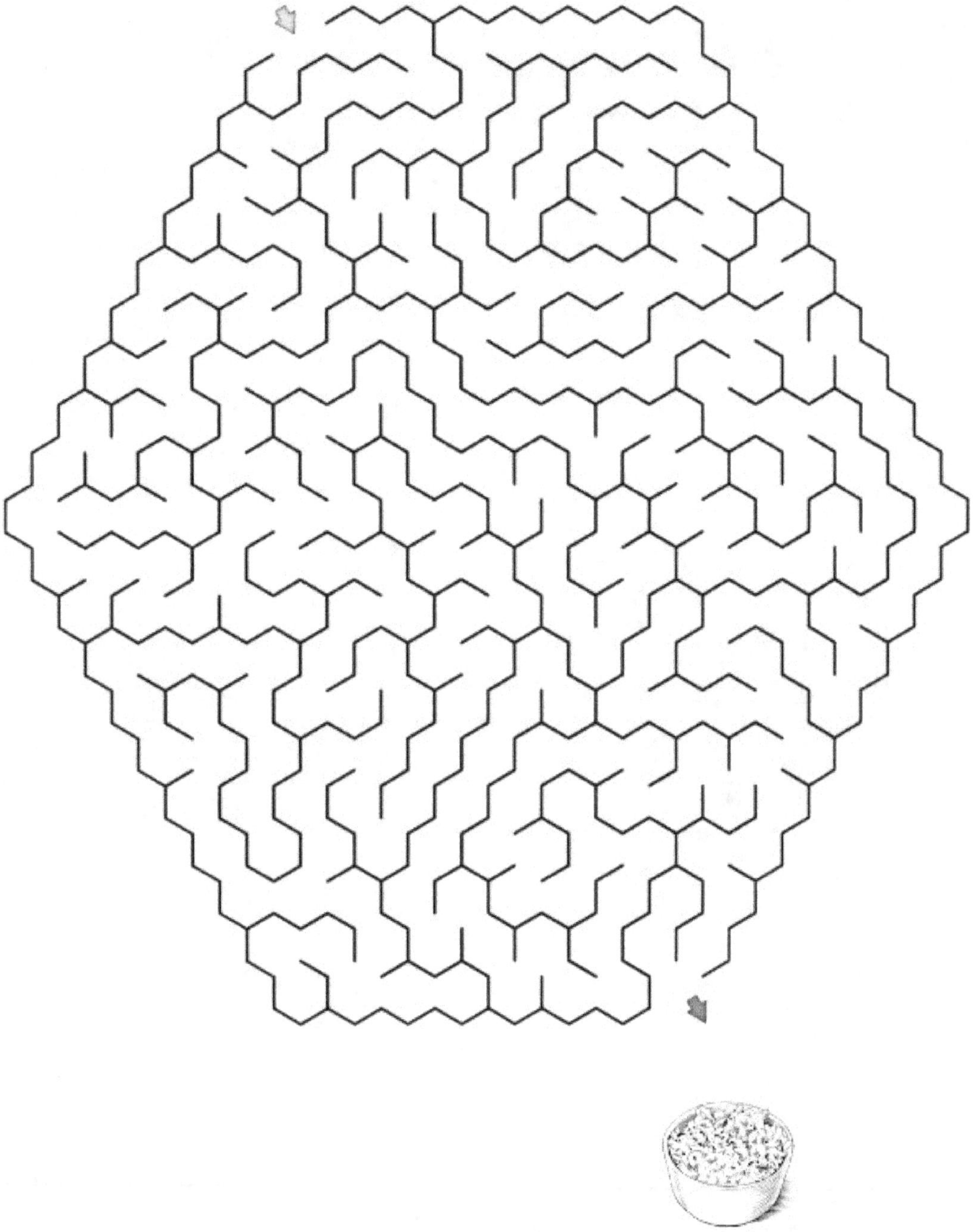

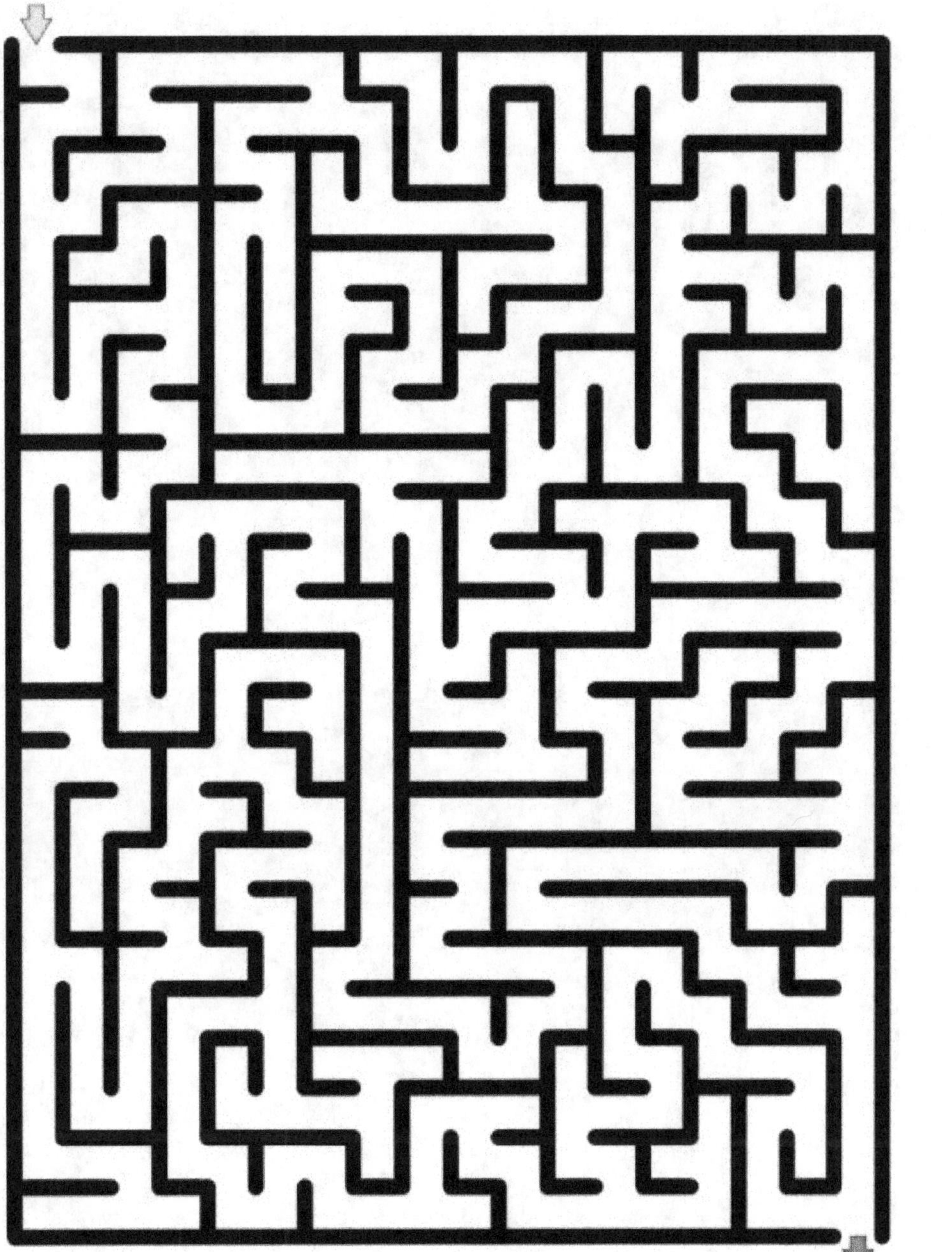

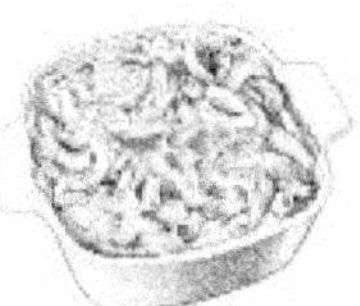

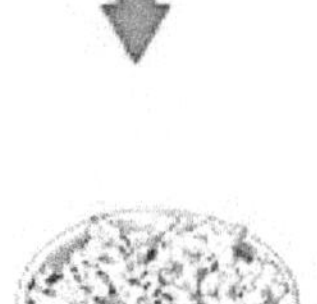

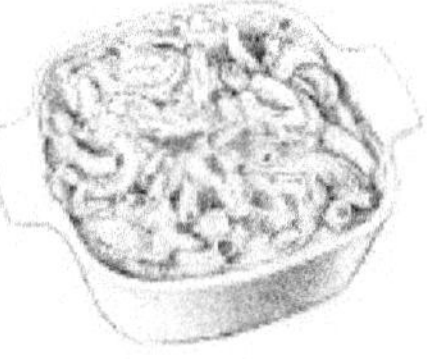

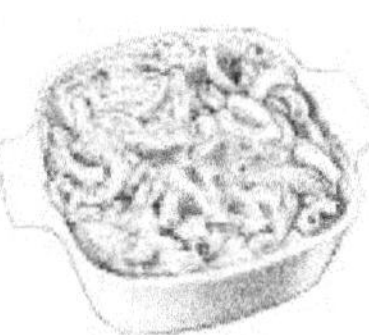